BORN TO SUCCEED

The Secret Code to a Successful Life

Dr. Varinder Mann

Published by
Hasmark Publishing International
www.hasmarkpublishing.com

Disclaimer

This book is designed to provide information and motivation to our readers. It is sold with the understanding that the publisher is not engaged to render any type of psychological, legal, or any other kind of professional advice. The content of each article is the sole expression and opinion of its author, and not necessarily that of the publisher. No warranties or guarantees are expressed or implied by the publisher's choice to include any of the content in this volume. Neither the publisher nor the individual author(s) shall be liable for any physical, psychological, emotional, financial, or commercial damages, including, but not limited to, special, incidental, consequential or other damages. Our views and rights are the same: You are responsible for your own choices, actions, and results.

Permission should be addressed in writing to Dr. Varinder Mann at manndvm37@gmail.com

Editor: Allison Burney
allison.burney@gmail.com

Cover and Book Design: Anne Karklins, Kelly Kinsman
anne@hasmarkpublishing.com

ISBN 13: 978-1-989756-27-0
ISBN 10: 1989756271

This book is dedicated to my parents, who always encouraged me to follow my dreams, and to my wife and beautiful daughters, who suggested the writing of these successful habits which made me wealthy and successful. Their continuing inspiration and support will keep me SUCCESSFUL and wealthy eternally.

This book is also dedicated to all the great motivational and inspiring people from whom I learnt and am still learning from each day about this beautiful life. They've taught me how to empower my mind to live life fully, without any inhibition. Some of my favorite teachers are Bob Proctor, Jack Canfield, Jim Rohn, Tony Robbins, Dr. Maxwell Maltz, Napoleon Hill, Zig Ziglar, Oprah Winfrey, Earl Nightingale, Dr Wayne Dyer and Robin Sharma. Thank you so much for guiding me on this beautiful path to a successful, happy, healthy, wealthy and self-fulfilled life.

Own your disciplines, elevate your life.
Disciplines set your life on autopilot to health,
happiness, wealth and prosperity.
– Dr. Mann

CONTENTS

CHAPTER ONE

———————

What Success Means to You

Successful people leave foot-prints, if you follow them,
it will lead you to a successful path.

I am writing this book based on my experience about life: how to live life beautifully, abundantly, happily, successfully, and with great passion for what I am going through. I have never been a writer and never imagined that one day I'd be writing. People have told me that writers are born with talent. That's what I thought all my life, whenever I thought of putting something on paper and sharing it with the world. This inferiority complex, low self-esteem and false beliefs held me down. Still, my deep desire and my intuition told me to write down all the little things that helped me to live a successful and wealthy life, and I listened.

Whenever my heart felt like writing something, I got pulled back by all the thoughts and people's opinions about being a writer. I just thought, *there's no way I can be a writer!* People have always told me that I explain things well and tell an interesting story. Some suggested I write a book, but I still had that fear that I could never be a writer, as I don't know how to express things well on paper. Then someone came into my life – the most beautiful, most wonderful person I've ever met. This person saw something in my writing. She saw talent that could be used to write, so she told me to write something.

This book is for her, since she encouraged me to write this. She inspired me so much that I can't explain how I felt. I just got very confident about my writing. My writing is for her. It's a small act, considering all her support and courage, and everything she's done for me. The person I'm talking about here is my beautiful, loving, caring and supportive WIFE. I couldn't have written this without her. Thank you, my love, for always being there for me, and for supporting me and encouraging me to write and express what's in my heart.

One day I made up my mind to put all my life experiences on paper and to put all my lessons in writing. When I started on this path, I always wondered why some people are so successful in life and others, like me, are living an average, mediocre life. What's the secret of their success? Why do successful people have everything they desire? On the other hand, why do average people like me have to think twice about buying something, planning a vacation, or treating myself to a restaurant meal? Then I started searching for success. After deep searching and researching success, the question came:

What is success?

To tell you the truth, at the time, my definition of success was having more money. I was under the impression that when I had more money, I'd be successful – but that was not the case. Money doesn't bring success. It's actually the other way around. When you are successful, money will follow you. When you are successful in your profession (whatever profession you're in), you won't have any scarcity of money. Each person has their own definition of success. I know yours is probably different than mine. I'm not saying that's wrong. We're all right, because that's what our success means. Different people have different definitions of success. Some consider doing what they love to do in their life the moment they wake up to be success. Some consider having wealth and tons of money to be success. Some consider having a beautiful soulmate to spend their life with – their dream partner – to be success. Some consider it their amazing, wonderful, loving family. Some consider it traveling.

In my view, success is having abundance in every area of your life: your job, a beautiful, loving partner, your loving, caring, and supportive family, travel, an abundance of spirituality, living the luxurious life, a connection with the infinite power within you, and good health. Success means balance in everything: money, health, wealth, prosperity, joy and spirituality.

The best definition of success I came across was while I was reading *The Strangest Secret* by Earl Nightingale. He said, "Success is the progressive realization of worthy ideals." He mentions that you're successful if you're doing what you love doing. If you want to be a teacher and you are teaching, then you're successful. If you want to be a doctor and are treating patients and making a difference in their lives, you're successful. If you're not doing what you want to be doing, then you aren't successful. Noah Webster defined success as "the successful accomplishment of a goal sought for." Some people confuse success with having all the material things. I would encourage you to consider *being successful* rather than success. Human beings are always looking for their goals, and move in their direction, according to how God has made them. It's in their system to operate that way. True success is if you are moving toward your goal or the direction you want to move, and are self-fulfilled. Real success for anyone is when they enjoy what they are doing. Both true success and happiness embrace each other; where one is found, the other will follow automatically.

When I was young, I always wanted to be a veterinarian. I wanted to treat animals and make them feel well. I believed that making a pet well and free from pain not only made a difference in the pet's life, but also their owner's, as they are all family members. I'm grateful for what I'm doing. I love my profession and feel accomplished. Since that was what I wanted to be, I consider myself successful. This is the main reason for writing this book. I want to tell everybody the little things I did on a day-to-day basis that made me successful. There are so many people stuck in their lives and circumstances that they don't see any way out. If you are feeling that way, you're on the right track reading this book. There are simple and easy day-to-day basics that will help you be successful in all areas of your life. To be happy and successful in life, you must follow successful habits or disciplines like the wealthiest and most successful have. To be successful, you must pay the price and put the work in. Nature's law states that whatever you put in will come back to you. In actuality, you receive so much more in return than what you put in. Whatever you sow, you reap. These daily habits and rituals will make a difference in your life if you do them with faith, persistence and concentration. These rituals shape your future on a daily basis. It's not just a one time thing – you have to practice and follow these every day. The daily disciplines I share in this book helped me to become a millionaire, and to become healthy and abundant in all areas of my life. They're very easy to do, but at the same time, they're not. If I can do it, anybody can. We're all born with beautiful, powerful minds which can help us achieve anything in life if we practice these disciplines daily with strong belief. I follow these daily rituals the moment I get up in the morning and the moment my head touches the pillow at night. I've been doing this for less than two years and my life is totally different. I'm living in my dream house, I'm financially sound, and I'm traveling with my family to our dream locations. Whatever I dreamt before starting on this path, it's become reality by following G.O.D. (Genius of Disciplines). I'm now wealthy, healthy and enjoying life to the fullest, traveling wherever I want to. I'm financially free.

I'm going to tell you what I do on a daily basis without leaving anything out. It was the persistence of these daily habits that turned my life into a beautiful, successful, financially free life. You'll begin to receive the same benefits (or more) if you follow these easy-to-do daily habits with persistence, faith, belief and concentration. Life is beautiful, and it has everything one desires, but you have to decide what you want. Life is abundant in every aspect and has plenty to offer, but you must know how to get what you want. There are rules of life. You can learn the rules to operate life on your terms by deciding what you really want. Nobody can decide this for you. Only you can choose what really matters to you. How do you want to live your life? What things do you want to have, and what will make you happy? These are the simple, daily habits that changed my life forever. I call them G.O.D. (Genius of Disciplines). I know and am sure that all successful people follow the same daily rituals to succeed in life, as succeeding in life is not about doing something once or getting lucky. It's about doing something small every day. Small, positive habits make you succeed in life and put you on the path to health, wealth, success, joy, harmony and prosperity. G.O.D. helped me achieve everything in life and made me live a successful, happy, healthy life, and I'm sure it will help you achieve and live your dream life.

Human beings are God's highest creation. He wants you to succeed and enjoy everything on this earth. You are:

– born to succeed

– born to have everything you can think of

– born to be rich

– born to be happy

– born to have a self-fulfilled life

– born to be free

– born to be financially free

– born to live successfully

You have everything within you. You have unlimited powers within you, unlimited resources to uncover, and unlimited capabilities. You can do anything you put your mind to. If you look around, you'll see that everything is in excess. Look at nature. Nature has no inhibition. Trees won't stop growing. Fruit never grows half-size. Water does not flow halfway. Birds don't just fly a little bit. All of nature is full of abundance, everywhere. It's the same way in human beings. The only thing that stops human beings from growing is their limiting beliefs. You have to let your mind work freely in accordance with nature's law. Whatever you want to achieve, start working toward it. The only way you can achieve everything is by taking action. Start today, and live the life of your dreams by becoming the person you want to become. You have nothing to lose – but a beautiful, amazing, wonderful, self-fulfilled dream life to WIN!

CHAPTER TWO

Disciplines Pave the Way to Success

The only difference between successful and average people is that successful people have certain disciplines which they follow daily. These disciplines are the secret of their success. I've met so many successful people, and each of them has certain disciplines that they incorporated into their life which made them a success over a period of time. They all give credit to these daily disciplines for making them successful. In my opinion, discipline is the one thing you need to live fully and abundantly. The key factor in reaching and achieving a successful life is discipline. Once you start using this key idea of discipline in your life, you won't see it the same way. Discipline and patience go hand in hand. Without patience, you cannot get disciplined. Discipline is the key to a healthy, wealthy, prosperous and happy life. In every area of life, nothing is possible without discipline.

Discipline:

– is the core of a good life

– is the secret of a wonderful and fulfilled life

- is possible by being patient

- changes every aspect of your life

- is the only and most important key for real success in life

The major key to success is not gathering knowledge, learning the traits of a business, or cluttering your mind with everything in this world. You have seen that most people have great knowledge, but their lives are not fulfilled. They are not living their dream life. They know more than anybody, but without application. Why are those people wandering aimlessly and living an average life, rather than their dream, self-fulfilled life? Have you ever asked yourself and wondered why? Everybody has different answers to this basic question of why these intelligent people are not living to their calibre, but the fundamental answer is the lack of discipline in their life. If you want to achieve and live a successful life, you have to incorporate discipline in your life. There is no way to sugar-coat why discipline is important in achieving success in life. It's the fundamental key to a great, fulfilling life, which everybody wants to live. Some people call discipline a trans-formational ritual, and once it's incorporated into life, it will bring transformation beyond anticipation. On the other hand, lack of discipline will cause loss of credibility. Most of the time, we know everything about what will help us transform our lives, but we fail to take any action. If you have gathered knowledge, but you are not taking any action to proceed further, it's useless. It's not going to benefit you in any way, whether it's financially, in relationships, or in any other endeavor. Discipline will help you to succeed in life.

It will:

- help you improve your relationship with your spouse
  or kids or other family members

- help you be more productive in your day-to-day work through better time management
- make you more healthy through regular workouts
- help you excel in your studies by spending time learning daily
- make you a better person who is more kind, patient, and grateful

Now, the question is, how will discipline help you in the ways mentioned above? If you discipline yourself to exercise daily, it will definitely help you become more healthy. If you are more healthy, you'll be more energetic and attentive in your day-to-day activities, whether at work, spending time with your family, or devoting time to self-care. In my opinion, discipline is beneficial at any age. It doesn't matter whether you are a kid, an adult or a senior. If you start living a disciplined life at an early age, your ride will be smoother and easier as time goes on. Even if you started late, don't worry. It will benefit you in so many different ways beyond your anticipation. I also realized the importance of discipline in shaping a successful life past forty. Since I started doing these daily disciplines or rituals, the rewards I am getting are much more than what I am putting in. A few disciplines are bringing multiple rewards for me since I adopted this strategy. Try to discipline yourself in whatever field you want to achieve success in. I promise you the rewards will be exponential and beyond your expectation. Discipline will definitely pave your path to a successful, prosperous, healthy, wonderful, and happy life. Discipline is not easy, but it is simple. Discipline is a full-time activity, as you have to do things on a consistent basis. Discipline also changes your philosophy about life. You start feeling better and start thinking better and do great things. I learned from Jim Rohn that success is not about something you pursue; it's something you attract by living a disciplined life. Discipline opens the door to a self-fulfilling life. Start doing daily disciplines in your life, and you will astonish yourself by achieving success beyond your dreams.

I am going to discuss the simple daily rituals or practices which I am doing on a consistent basis that totally changed my life for good. When I started doing these little rituals every day, I didn't know they would empower my life and earn me great wealth and health, and fulfill my dreams of obtaining a perfect and happy life. When I started doing these rituals, I was enjoying my life and had no idea these rituals would turn my life around for the better. I was working a nine to five job for the federal government. You might think this kind of job is safe, sound and secure, and that your life is set. You have a great pension in retirement. I started reading self-help books from motivational speakers and didn't dream that it would be good for me. After achieving success in life, I know that anybody can succeed if they want to. Success is boring and hard work, and hard work means you have to continue on a consistent basis, even when your mind asks you why you are doing it. *Give up*, it says. But you don't have to. Keep going, even when it seems hard and impossible. Every mistake and every failure will bring you one step closer to your destination. These are not difficult disciplines. They're easy, simple day-to-day rituals that anybody can perform and succeed.

Once you incorporate daily consistent disciplines in your life, then you have to believe that these disciplines will take you to your dream life. Start with little disciplines, like reading 10 minutes of a self-help motivational book, or working out for 15 minutes. Go for a 10-minute jog, or start by putting a hundred dollars into a savings account. Small disciplines will make you stronger day by day.

CHAPTER THREE

Believe and Succeed

"You have to believe in yourself when no one else does. That's what makes you a winner."

– Venus Williams,
Olympic gold medalist and professional tennis champion

I will explain all the rituals I've been doing. I'm a hundred percent sure it will make a difference in your life if you'll just follow them with an open mind and fully believe in yourself. "Believing is seeing," as Napoleon Hill said.

If your mind can believe and conceive, it can achieve.

What is belief? How can you embed belief in yourself to achieve success in life? Belief is the key to achieving anything in life. If you believe you can do it, chances are pretty good that you will achieve your desire, as long as you have strong belief in yourself. Belief is having conviction that what you think will become reality. Belief is the most important step in every stage of life, and it will help you at any stage of life. It doesn't matter where you are in life currently. It does not matter:

- whether you are broke, and want to become wealthy
- whether you are weak, and want to become strong
- whether you are sick, and want to feel better
- whether you are not doing well in your studies, and want better grades
- whether you have failed in business, and want to become successful

In all of these cases, you have to take action in order to proceed in life. The most important step is to believe in yourself that you can do it. You have the ability to succeed at whatever you want to achieve. You must have strong and unwavering belief in your very own capabilities. As far as I know, human beings are God's highest and greatest creation in the universe. Human beings were given unique and magical powers, just like God. God intended every human being to succeed in life, whether you're a doctor, engineer, lawyer, high school dropout, or housewife. Whatever your status may be, God's vision and purpose is for human beings to become great and successful in whatever profession they set their hearts and minds to. It is also God's vision that human beings enjoy each and every aspect of the good in the universe. Human beings are born to be successful, to be rich, and to have the best in the universe. Each human is born unique. No one is exactly the same. We all have different fingerprints, different faces, and different qualities. You can't find someone exactly like yourself in this world. What makes you so different?

- You are special
- You are unique
- You are talented

– You have everything within you

You have everything you could imagine, but you have to properly develop and scientifically apply these qualities to ensure success and true joy in your life. You are made to learn and progress. You ought to succeed; that is what God wants for each and every human being on this earth. Everybody has great power within themselves. You awaken the power through psychological methods such as self-help, self-discovery, and most importantly, belief in yourself. As Henry Ford once said, "If you think you can or cannot, either way you are right." Begin believing in yourself. Do you wish to succeed? I'm sure you want to – that's why you are reading this book. How can you believe in yourself? What are the methods to embed a successful, never-ending belief system? How was our old belief system embedded in the first place? One thing I do on a daily basis is repeat affirmations in whatever I want to achieve: "I believe, I believe, I believe."

Our belief system came from our surroundings, our environment, our parents, our society and our close relatives. From birth, everything we're exposed to creates our belief system. If you are raised in a poor community, chances are very good that your mind is conditioned to poverty. If, on the other hand, you are raised in a high-end community, your mind is conditioned to prosperity. I'm not talking about everyone; there are some exceptions around who has ambition to do something in life. Old belief systems play a major part in our results in life. In order to change your life, you have to change your belief system.

You can change your belief system by:

1. Repeating affirmations with conviction

When you say affirmations every day, after some time, your brain thinks they are true. Then you start seeing results in your life according to what you chant every day to yourself. I changed my belief system by using affirmations as a key weapon against my old, self-sabotaging belief system. My favorite affirmations, which totally changed my life, are:

"I am a genius and apply my wisdom."

"Day by day, in every way, I am getting better and better."

I repeat these affirmations a couple of times a day and at night. They are so embedded in my subconscious mind that I am seeing and experiencing the results every day.

2. Reading self-help and motivational books

My favorite list of books are:

Think and Grow Rich by Napoleon Hill

Psycho-Cybernetics by Maxwell Maltz

The Magic of Thinking Big by David J. Schwartz

Success Principles by Jack Canfield

Awaken the Giant Within by Tony Robbins

There are many more, and the list goes on. I am a voracious reader, and reading totally changed my perceptive on life for good. Reading great books also influences you and your belief system.

3. Connecting with like-minded people

The company you keep is important. You become what you hang around with. Environment plays a crucial role in shaping your destiny. What you think about, you become.

4. Listening to inspiring audio and watching motivational videos

5. Reading autobiographies of successful people

6. Visualizing the person you want to become

All of the above methods are simple, but not easy. Anybody can try these methods and change their life. If I can change my life by adopting these methods, so can you.

Change Your Self-image, Change Your Life

Another important aspect which helped me to change my belief system was changing my self-image. You must be wondering, what is self-image? Self-image and beliefs go hand in hand. They both work simultaneously, and if you change one, the other will change automatically. Self-image is the most important discovery of the century, and totally changed the perspective of the psychology of human beings. It was first promulgated by Dr. Maxwell Maltz, who was a renowned plastic surgeon in the early 1960s. Your belief system that you got unconsciously from past experiences, past failures, other people, and past successes will either impair or make your self-image. Self-image is what you think of yourself and what kind of picture you are holding in your mind of yourself. If you change your belief system by the methods mentioned above, indirectly you are changing your self-image. Self-image is definitely the golden key in living a successful life. What you think of yourself has a huge impact on your life, and decides whether you live like a wealthy, successful person, or like a pauper. If you are holding a self-image of a wealthy, successful person, you would naturally be living like that, and vice versa. Your actions, behaviors, thoughts, and feelings are always consistent with whatever you are holding as your self-image. Self-image is the seed of a successful life. If you want to change the plant or fruit, you have to change the seed accordingly. You can't grow an apple tree from an orange seed, in the same way that you can't carry a self-image of failure if you want to succeed in life.

When I was growing up, I was holding a self-image of failure. I was in the company of like-minded people, and those were the results I was seeing in my life. Since I slowly changed my self-image by thinking and imagining myself successful, my life is better. I have plenty of money and my business is booming. Every day I see more opportunities and get rewarded beyond my anticipation. If you want to change your life, you cannot change the circumstances. The only thing you can change is yourself, by changing your self-image. When you change the picture of yourself in your mind, all the things related to your self-image will be changed without any effort. Most people try to change the outside world in order to achieve success, but that's similar to changing your picture in the mirror without changing your physical appearance. It's futile and not going to happen, no matter how hard you try.

If you want to change your life, you have to change your self-image. Are you ready for your journey to success? Let's go for this wonderful ride by following these simple things, which are not always easy to do.

CHAPTER FOUR

Make Your Destiny by Thinking About What You Want

What do you really WANT?

The first time I heard the question, "What do you really want?" was when I attended a paradigm shift seminar in Los Angeles. It was the first thing Bob Proctor mentioned in his opening speech. Most people in this world don't really know what they want. Take my life as an example. All my life, I was working hard and trying to achieve – but I had no idea what I really wanted until this seminar. I was shooting arrows into the dark, unsure of my target. If you don't know what your target is, there's a pretty good chance that you aren't going to hit it. If you want success and want to live your dream life, you must first decide what you really want.

When you ask most people what they want, they answer vaguely:

"I want plenty of money."

"I want more freedom."

"I want rest."

"I want to travel more."

"I want a high-paying job."

"I want my dream partner."

They are hardly specific on anything. "More money" is very vague. Do they want pennies, or a dollar bill? I was guilty of this too before I started doing these daily rituals consistently. Then I realized that I had to really decide what I wanted in my life. Once I made up my mind and decided what I wanted, these things really started rolling into my life, to my surprise. Decide what you want. Take the first step on this beautiful journey and decide what really matters to you and what you really, truly want in your life. You HAVE to be specific in describing what you want. I love Bob Proctor's famous quote that he mentions in his seminar and on his website:

"If you know what you want, I will show you how to get it!"

You have to decide what you really want. Think for a few moments right now and decide. Write down what you really want. I always ask everyone I meet what they want. To my surprise, and also to my sadness, people don't know what they want. They have no idea what that means. They get confused when I ask them, and I'm astonished at the expressions on their faces. It's like I asked them some forbidden question. I'm not saying this is their fault; it's not their fault because they don't know how this works. They're not sure what they want and why they are not getting anywhere in life. Research tells us that only 5 percent of the people in the world know what they want, and that same 5 percent of people earn 95 percent of the money in the world. I've heard it said that if you were to divide all the money in the world into equal parts among all the people of the world, sooner or later that same five percent of people will have the same amount of money they did before. How is that possible? Because that five percent of people know what they want! Your mind works according to the clarity of your vision and your ambition. The clearer you are on your vision, the easier and the sooner your mind will bring it to you. You have to be clear about your definiteness of purpose in life. According to Napoleon Hill, "Definiteness of purpose is the starting point of all achievement. That's why successful people move on their own initiative. They know where they are going before they begin. That's why they are successful. They know their journey of life with definiteness of purpose by deciding and being clear on what they really want." When you know and have decided what you really want, you'll get clear on your vision and then things start falling into place. When you decide your vision and what you really want in your life, your subconscious mind starts working towards that and will bring it into your life.

Since I learned from Bob Proctor that the first thing I had to do was decide what I wanted, I did that, and just by being clear on my definiteness of purpose, I achieved my goals in a very short period of time. I made this practice my daily routine. It's a lifelong process. Once you get a hold of this wonderful secret to decide what you want, you'll achieve anything in your life that you focus your mind on. As Steve Covey told us, it's possible to do more in a short period of time with less effort. I was very happy and very surprised that by doing these simple daily rituals, I achieved my goal and became successful very quickly. I knew I needed to share the secret of my success with the world. There are people who are stuck and don't see any light in their life. They're working hard and they're sincere, but they're struggling. I want to help people like you achieve whatever you want to achieve in life, whether it's related to money, health, wealth or prosperity. By doing these simple acts, you can live abundantly in all aspects of life. Don't waste a single second wandering aimlessly. Start thinking about what you really want now.

Decide. Decide, Decide, Decide, Right Now, What You Want:

Is more money what you want?

Is wealth what you want?

Is financial freedom what you want?

Is a change of career what you want?

Is finding your dream partner what you want?

Is raising your kids well and teaching them great values what you want?

Is having a great and understanding relationship with your spouse what you want?

Is more happiness what you want?

Is traveling to all the exotic places in the world what you want?

Is helping your parents in their retirement what you want?

Is helping your siblings what you want?

Is owning your own business what you want?

Is winning a gold medal in the Olympics what you want?

Is self-fulfillment what you want?

The time to decide is now, and the only thing that matters is what you want. Decide now. As I explained, this is one of the most important lessons I learned. It helped me achieve wealth, prosperity, abundance, harmony and joy in my life. You can have the same things in your life. If I can do it, you can too!

Don't wait. Decide today by writing down what you want. Let your subconscious mind help you to find happiness, health, wealth, and abundance by working on your clear vision of life. Be definite in what you want.

CHAPTER FIVE

Goals Can Help You Get Whatever You Want

"The pull of written goals works like MAGIC."

A very important step in your life is to ask for what you really want. Asking is the first and most important step. I wrote all my goals on an index card – and not just financial goals. I wrote my personal goals, my professional goals, my travel goals, my health and fitness goals, my behavioral goals (habits I wanted to change which were not helping me towards my goals), and material things.

This is an outline of my day:

Every day when I first wake up, before I step out of bed, I go over my goal cards. You don't have to write on an index card; you can write all your goals in your smartphone. Phones are easy to use and convenient. Most of us keep our smartphone with us all the time. People who don't want to write in their smartphone can write their goals on an index card. In the morning, read all your goals with good feelings. See yourself already achieving that goal or living the life you want to live. In the morning, your mind is fresh and quiet, and more prone to accepting the ideas. It hasn't been bombarded yet by all the hectic things going on due to your work, your personal life, issues, etc.

Asking about your goals from a higher power is an important first step toward a rich, joyful, serene, happy and abundant life. If you're not sure about what you want to do, chances of getting anywhere are zero. It's just like when you're traveling somewhere: if you don't know where you want to go, how can you end up at your destination? If you come out of your driveway without knowing where you're going, you'll wander around aimlessly. Life works the same way. If you don't know what you want to do, you'll wander aimlessly and not gain the success you desire. If you don't have goals, you won't succeed. If you ask any person what their goals are, most people will look at you, like, "What you are talking about?"

I was also like this. I didn't have any goals. I looked at successful people or met successful people and wanted to become like them, but I had no idea how to get there. If you ask any successful person the secret of their success, they can tell you how they get there. I did not have any written goals, and that's why, for so many years, I wandered aimlessly.

It's G.O.D. (Genius of Disciplines) that will change you from where you are to where you want to be. Daily habits that you do every day will get you there. Daily habits condition your mind to the good things in your life. For example, if you want to earn more money, you have to condition your mind to accept money, and you have to think abundantly before you actually see it in your reality. In order to condition your mind, you have to study money, wealth and success. Successful people all have their minds conditioned to money. They always think abundantly and get abundance in their life. To condition your mind to abundance, you have to think about how rich and successful people live, what their lifestyle is like, how they walk, how they talk, how they behave, and what their daily routines are. When I was thinking about succeeding in life and didn't have any idea how to achieve whatever I wanted, I started asking my higher power by writing my goals on a card. I began speaking them out loud every day first thing in the morning. I started visualizing what my life would be like when I achieved my goals. This helped me raise my vibration to one that felt really good.

The universe operates on vibration. Whatever you feel, you'll attract. Once your goals are written, it means they belong to you. If you can think of your goals in your mind, you'll definitely manifest them in your life. Make up your mind. You can have whatever your heart desires, because whatever you desire is waiting for you. Everything in this universe is waiting for you – you just have to mentally tap into it and claim it. Don't worry and don't let fear hold you back. It's your fear that's standing between you, your goals and your success in life. Fear is in everybody's life. Everyone is afraid of something. Some are fearful of heights. Some fear daily life situations, and some are fearful of health. Some people fear losing loved ones, and some are fearful of rejection. It's natural. Let your problems go by focusing on the things you want. Don't focus on what you don't want. We always attract people like us because we're on the same frequency. Stretch yourself mentally by thinking every day about what you want to achieve. Think of the best thing that can happen to you today in any area of your life. Think about that for a moment and let your mind relax. What's the best thing that can happen to you today? Relaxation of the mind is very important for infinite intelligence to flow through you and give you ideas.

Successful people who have done excellent work are just ordinary people like us who are doing extraordinary things. They accomplish this by relaxing their mind with simple relaxation techniques like meditation. If you want to win in your life, you have to relax, because then a higher power flows through you, as James Allen said in his marvelous little book, *As a Man Thinketh*. Calmness of the mind is one of the beautiful jewels of wisdom. It's the result of long and patient efforts in self-control. Its presence is an indication of ripened experience, and of more than ordinary knowledge of the laws and operations of thought.

Let's talk about goals. When I first heard about goals, I didn't understand what it meant. When Bob Proctor asked everybody about their goals, I thought, *WHAT?* But he was right. If you don't have any goals, you're not living your life to the fullest. As he always says, God made man his highest creation. God wants man to enjoy everything in life, and have everything he can think of. He doesn't want his highest creation to live in scarcity and misery. Most people don't have any goals and may not even know what goals are. They simply haven't been taught this. Everybody should have goals. If you don't have goals and you don't know where you want to go, you're going to end up at somebody else's destination.

According to me, setting goals means getting your ambitions and desires on paper. Goals are like a GPS: they guide you to where you're going. When you're clear about your goals and desires, you're excited about working toward them. Once you put your goals on paper, the pull of your destination becomes stronger and stronger if your vision is CLEAR. Goals help you grow. Suppose your goal is becoming a millionaire. I know you can definitely achieve that goal if you really want to. I know everybody wants to hit this jackpot goal, but my point is that it's not the million dollars that matters – it's the person you become to achieve that million dollars that's worth multi-millions. That's how goals work; they stretch you beyond your limits to be the best person you can be. Once you've achieved any goal in your life, you won't be the same person as you were when you started. Achieving your goal forever changes you, both personally and mentally. It's this change which makes you a confident, successful person.

As I learned from Bob Proctor, there are three categories of goals.

Types of Goals:

1. Goals that you practice every day

These are things you're achieving without much effort on your part. These goals come to your life routinely. For example, let's say you tell me your goal is to buy a new Mercedes. I ask you what kind of car you drive now, and you tell me a four-year-old Mercedes that you've been driving for four years. This is not a goal you need my help with. You already know how to achieve this.

2. Goals you think you can achieve

If you have a goal you feel you can achieve easily, you won't be motivated and inspired to work on it. I don't think these goals are worth it. It's much better to set goals that you need to stretch your mind to achieve. You need to think out of the box when you're achieving goals. For example, if I'm planning to buy a house a bit bigger than my current house, I don't have to think about this; I can just do what I did to buy this house. There's no growth here and no stretching your mind.

3. Fantasy Goals

Many people don't fantasize. They think fantasies are for

kids. As we get older, we think we have to face reality and fantasy has no place in our lives. When we think that, our conscious mind gives us more reasons not to fantasize. People think things are impossible and aren't going to happen. As we get older, our minds get adulterated by our circumstances and we don't think the way we used to when we were kids. We used to fantasize about everything. We've become ignorant and don't know the power of mind. Our mind is the most beautiful, most powerful organ we humans possess. It's the only thing that separates us from animals. Animals don't have the power of imagination. They're comfortable in their environment, and they can't change their environment even if they want to. But as humans, we can change our outer circumstances and our environment if we choose. We have the power to do it. Humans are remarkable, and they can do remarkable things in life. We don't appreciate or value the price of our beautiful mind. Anything that comes to us without any price has no value; but in reality, anything that comes to our life free is priceless.

These goals are really out of the box; they are our dream life. The first obstacle we have to face is our inner fear. We don't have to think about how we can achieve this, we just have to let our subconscious mind take care of it. Write down your goal once you've decided on it. Some people have goals in mind, but they never write them down. Writing them down is the first piece of manifestation. Writing your goals on paper and reading them aloud every day is very important, and helps you achieve the goal. Carry your goal card (or your phone) with you everywhere you go. When you carry your goals, be sure to read them during the day. Your beautiful mind will bring all the situations and circumstances around you to help you make your goals reality. Set fantasy goals which will blow your mind when you achieve them and stretch you as a human being. These are goals that put you on the path to abundance, freedom, financial freedom and happiness. Write your goals on paper and read them aloud every morning and before bed. This embeds your goals in your subconscious mind and your life will never be the same. I am using this technique for all my goals and seeing the results every day. This simple goal-setting technique will put you on the path to your dream life. Don't wait! Start working toward your dream life from this moment on!

CHAPTER SIX

Gratitude is the Real Magic in Your Life

Be thankful.

Gratitude is the easiest thing in life to express. You have to be grateful for little things in your life, like getting a parking spot. Always say thanks to your higher power. When you're grateful for small things in life, it connects you to the infinite power in the universe. When you're not grateful, you break the connection to your infinite power which gives you all these things to be grateful for. According to Wallace Wattles in *The Science of Getting Rich*, "If the only thing you say in your life is 'Thank You,' that is more than sufficient. Gratitude opens the door to success, wisdom, intelligence, happiness, love, affection and abundance. If you are grateful for every little thing in your life, you will end up having more and more in your life."

Gratitude is one of the most beautiful and amazing secrets I ever learned. Since I started following that ritual, I am getting everything in my life. I have more and more to be grateful for. My life totally changed and all the changes are phenomenal.

I never thought this simple gratitude exercise would bring so much wealth, abundance and prosperity into my life. My gratitude ritual is to say thank you more than 100 times a day. In the morning before getting out of bed, I say thank you. When my feet touch the ground, I say thank you. While brushing my teeth, I say thank you. "Thank you" creates many beautiful, loving, and positive vibrations around you. This brings more and more things and circumstances in your life to be grateful for. Even when you find a penny on the road or in a parking lot, pick it up and say thank you to the Universe for giving this money to you.

I always find time during the day to say thank you. My gratitude drive is another ritual that's worked wonders for me. While I drive to work in the morning, I say thank you for something in my life at each red light I hit. It not only makes me feel good first thing in the morning, but it also ensures that I begin my day on a positive note. Initially, it was very hard to remember while driving. Then I wrote "THANK YOU" on an index card and put it on my dashboard to remind me. Once I did this practice for 30 days, it became a habit. Now it's so embedded in my subconscious mind that whenever I'm driving somewhere, as soon as I hit a light, my mind starts chanting gratitude for the things in my life. Since I started this practice, I've been achieving all my goals and getting unexpected things to be grateful for every day. Gratitude is a real game-changer for me. My drive to work is about 18 miles, and I hit about 20 lights and say thank you 20 times. When you start doing something every day, it becomes your habit. When I hit a light, my subconscious mind automatically says thank you even if I'm not thinking about gratitude at all! Gratitude is the magic key to living a beautiful, happy, loving, wealthy and abundant life. When you feel gratitude in everything you do, all the beautiful, harmonious feelings help you achieve whatever goals you visualize or take action on. Even a simple repetition of "Thank You" several times a day with positive feelings and a harmonious state of mind will help you feel good, and bring prosperity, happiness and abundance. Everyone has the power to express gratitude, but not everybody knows how to use it. It's not rocket science to use the power of gratitude. It's very easy and is one of the most important powers we humans have. If all of us put this power into action with feelings of gratitude, everything in the world would be possible. For example, if you do something for your loved one and they appreciate it and say thank you, you'll feel like doing more acts of service for them. This works the same way in every aspect of life. When the higher power gives you something, whether it's money, time, material things, an award at work or school, or an 'A' on an exam, simply say thank you. You'll end up having more and more things to feel grateful for.

Another gratitude ritual I practice daily is gratitude writing. Every day, I write five things I'm grateful for in my gratitude journal. This exercise not only helps me find things I am grateful for, but at the same time, it helps me to think of good things that happened during the day. Thinking is the main power that drives human beings to success or failure. If you think happy, positive thoughts, your life will be happy and healthy. Sad, negative thoughts will make you miserable. These are simple day-to-day things I'm passing on to you. They're as simple as having a cup of tea or coffee in the morning. Starting a gratitude journal helps because in order to write, you have to think of things to be grateful for. When you start thinking about the good things, it changes your vibration. You feel good. Then you start attracting people and circumstances at that same frequency. You can write about what you already have and things you want to manifest in the future. Gratitude affirmations can also be written every day to totally change your life for the better.

You can use the examples here:

I am happy and grateful for…

I am healthy, wealthy and living an abundant life.

I am enjoying my life to the fullest.

I am enjoying my wonderful life with amazing, loving people.

I live in a beautiful, loving household.

I love money and money is good.

My wealth is multiplying every day.

I am grateful for another day on this earth and will put my best efforts forward today.

I am living a charmed life.

Thank you, God, for everything in my life.

I started practicing gratitude about a year ago. Since then, I've become healthy and wealthy, and am traveling to beautiful destinations I like and desire. Even while I'm writing this chapter on gratitude, I'm saying thank you. I cannot explain how great it feels to express gratitude. Try this simple practice and you'll be astonished at how it helps you in your business, your relationships, and with your happiness in general. I, too, wondered how this simple phrase could make any difference. When I started doing this ritual, I was struggling financially, my marriage was in trouble, and I wasn't happy at my job. When I started feeling gratitude, I opened my own practice, and it worked magic in my life. My marriage totally changed and became more loving. My relationship with my family improved, as did my finances.

I'd like to elaborate on how I started working on opening my own business. I was working a full-time job and wanted to open my own practice. The first thing I thought about was where will the money come from? When I started practicing gratitude and saying thank you every day, I ultimately found that the practice was already built, and I didn't have to spend any money to build it. The icing on the cake? The veterinarian who was running the practice had a conflict with the land-lord and had to leave the practice. When I found this out, I called the veterinarian. He encouraged me to start a practice at the same location where he'd been practicing. He told me it was one of the busiest locations for a veterinarian. This doctor offered me all his equipment for the practice at a nominal fee and gave me a whole year to pay! I know, it seems unbelievable. Gratitude totally changed my life. It worked magic and made me a millionaire.

Don't think that simply saying thank you for everything you have isn't going to do anything. Believe me, I thought this too – but this simple practice of gratitude opens the flood-gates to wealth, health, harmonious relationships, joy and prosperity. It brings miracles into your life. Don't wait to be grateful. Start this practice right this second! Once you start this practice, your life will be totally different in a short period of time. Like me, you'll be astonished to see the results. How did this happen? A higher power (or God) works in different times and different ways, which we humans can't figure out. If you ask me how this practice of gratitude works, I won't be able to explain it to you in detail. The only thing I can tell you from my experience is that this simple practice of grati-tude works, and it works wonders for everybody who uses it consistently, with faith and belief in themselves and in a higher power. Start saying thank you for everything you have and everything that's coming your way. Do it now. Don't wait for the perfect moment to be grateful. It's right here, right now. Give the command to yourself today, at this moment, to be grateful for everything in your life, and you'll see the flow of blessings come to you.

Be grateful for everything in your life!
Gratitude is the real magic formula I found by practice.

CHAPTER SEVEN

Your Words Are Your Real Gem of Life, So Use Them Wisely

Words are powerful!

The words we say to other people affect our lives in a big way. Before realizing the power of words, I never thought the words we speak could change our lives for good or bad. I'd be trying to get to work and saying to myself, "Oh, I'm stuck in traffic," and then other situations would make me more and more late. I didn't know the power of words or how this mind philosophy works. I was never rude, but I thought myself inferior and chanted low-frequency words until I read the wonderful book, *Your Word is Your Wand*, by Florence Scovel Shinn. It taught me the real power of words when we talk to people. It's true that whatever we say changes our feelings and thinking, even if you're not aware of it. If we speak negative words, either about ourselves or to or about other people, they create the same frequency of negativity. This, of course, attracts related situations and people of the same frequency, according to the law of attraction. Be very careful when you speak. Speak wisely.

It wasn't easy in the initial phases to speak consciously. We're all used to speaking without thinking. We say words all the time without even being aware of what we're saying and definitely not meaning what we say. Unless or until we're aware of our words, we can't speak with awareness. Most people aren't aware of what they're saying, so they don't have any idea why they are getting results they don't want. When they encounter a difficult situation or problem, they blame another person or circumstance for the difficulty. They don't realize it's because they've been chanting negativity all day long. I was also getting results I didn't want from saying negative things about myself and blaming others for my failures. I did this until I came to know that there's only one person responsible for my failures, life situation, and whatever I am today – and that's ME! Nobody else is responsible for my success or failure.

Once I became aware of the magic power of words, I started saying positive things about myself. I started chanting positive things and talking about some positive things I didn't have in the moment, but wanted to achieve. Within a short period of time, I started seeing results based on the things I was saying and thinking about all day. I was very surprised and shocked that for some reason, I was getting lucky all the time. The actual reason, though, is that I was using positive words in my daily routine. Now you know what kind of words you want to speak to yourself and others. You want to treat other people the way you want to be treated. Now I always speak positive words about myself and other people. It's not hard to do – but at the same time, it's not easy either. It's a daily routine. Once you set it up, it becomes automatic over time. Then the results are phenomenal. The exercise I do every day related to words is one I learned from Jack Canfield in his Seminar, "One Day to Greatness." Another exercise I do every day when I get up and before bed is what I call "The Self-appreciation exercise."

It goes like this:

Stand in front of the mirror and look into your eyes as you say the words below.

"Hello __________. (Use your name. That's very important. Always use your name). Good morning. I am so happy and grateful that I had a great sleep."

"Today I am going to have a beautiful and wonderful day."

Then I mention all my goals. You can say aloud with positive emotion (this is key!) all the goals you want to achieve and all your dreams. Talk about all the qualities you'd like to have and the person you want to become. For example, you can say:

"I am feeling happy and refreshed."

"I am healthy and wealthy."

"My wealth multiplies every day." (This is my favorite affirmation. Since I started doing it, my wealth IS multiplying every day and I'm seeing big changes in my bank balance!)

"Today is the perfect day and I give thanks for this beautiful, loving, abundant and miraculous day."

"Magic happens in my life and wonders shall never cease happening in my life."

Remember, starting the day with positive affirmations has a huge impact on your day. This is because in the morning, your mind is refreshed and free from any tension. Whatever you say goes directly to your subconscious mind. You feel energetic, happy and vibrant. These positive words set the tone of your day on a happy note.

When I started this exercise, it was very hard and emotional at the same time. I felt like I was talking to someone else, not to me. When I said affirmations about goals I hadn't achieved yet, my mind was telling me these were lies and I couldn't achieve them. Still, I continued for months, and once I started believing them, I saw results. For me, the magic that made this work was setting small short-term goals. As I fulfilled these small goals, my self-confidence skyrocketed and I started believing in myself more. Then I told myself, "If this is happening, anything I repeat to myself will come true." The exact same thing happened with all my big goals! They started appearing in my life without any hard work. For example, I wanted to own a mansion in California, and started affirming to myself the exact size of house I wanted. Within one year, I was living in that house.

In the morning, mainly, I talk about my goals with myself. Whatever my goals are, I try to feel the way I'll feel once my goal has been achieved. Suppose my goal is to have two million dollars in my bank account. I choose the exact date I'd like to have it. I start behaving the way I'll behave once I have the money. I say aloud, "I feel confident and wealthy, and I'm enjoying my life."

My morning prayer is usually some version of this:

"I am feeling very happy and energetic today.
My life is beautiful, and I am enjoying every bit of it.
My higher power is helping me solve any challenges
that show up today.
I always make wise decisions with
whatever knowledge I have.
I am living a charmed life.

*I am healthy, wealthy, prosperous and enjoying my life.
My day is filled with gratitude. All day long I am
thankful for everything in my life."*

This sets positive vibrations all around you, and you'll feel happy and look forward to your day. At night, before retiring for bed, I do an evening version of the "Self-appreciation" exercise. This exercise is very simple and very powerful in shaping your life. Again, stand in front of the mirror and look into your eyes as you say:

"Hello _________. (Say your name). I'd like to appreciate you for the day you had today. You did a great job working at your practice, doing all the surgeries safely and efficiently. You helped so many pets today. I appreciate you for dealing with all your clients and your employees with a caring, loving attitude. I appreciate that now you are going to bed on time. I love you so much. Thank you very much, _______. (You can use your name). You did an excellent job today. _________ (Say your name and be sure to look into your eyes), I LOVE YOU."

Loving yourself is the most important thing you can do. If you can't love yourself, you can't love anybody else. If you can't enjoy your own company, you'll never enjoy anybody else's. Your words are your gems. Use them with great caution and never use any negative, jealous words. By simply changing my words, my life and my attitude changed dramatically. I can now find solutions to any challenges I face very easily by simply using positive, empowering words.

Affirmations are very empowering. When you continuously repeat affirmations, initially it feels like you're lying. When you've done it for 30 days straight, you'll start feeling like this is your reality, and whatever you're asking for will start showing up. Remember to throw in some simple, easy-to-accomplish short-term goals. This helps with your belief. Once you accomplish some short-term goals, you'll have confidence about the larger, long-term ones.

Here's a great example of this principle in action with my daughter. She was nine years old and had just started wrestling in school.

She told me, "Dad, I want to win a trophy in wrestling."

"Let's do an affirmation," I told her.

She told me it wouldn't work because she's new at wrestling and other kids in her weight class are really good and would beat her. I told her to do the affirmation every day. She wanted to know if she'd get a trophy if she did the affirmation every day.

I told her, "Of course. 100 percent, you'll get it."

So, she started doing affirmations every day when I dropped her off at school. Within two or three months of her wrestling season, she progressed to the District level and ended up winning a trophy. What a beautiful gem to discover affirmations at such a young age! Now she does affirmations every day regarding her grades and she's doing very well, because kids believe very quickly. I'm so glad I taught this affirmation lesson to her. Her belief in affirmations is very grounded in her mind at age nine. She does all her affirmations every day during our short drive to her school. She decides her affirmations every day and tells me what they are. I'm so proud of her and grateful to the higher power for giving me the secret gem of affirmations. Don't wait any longer! Start this simple habit of saying good, positive words to yourself and everyone around you. Believe me, it will make your life more loving, more abundant, happy, prosperous and harmonious.

From today forward, make it your daily routine, even if you only say this one affirmation: "IT'S WORTH IT." Affirmations make your beautiful dreams come true! Be consistent with saying your affirmations and prayers every day. Try this new habit for 30 days. I promise you won't regret it and the results will be phenomenal. When you create your own affirmations, be sure they're in the present tense, easy and short.

CHAPTER EIGHT

Why Worry?
It May Never Happen in Your Life

Worry brings fear. Fear is devastating.

The main obstacle to your success and wealth is your habit of worrying. Fear is the biggest obstacle in your life. It will never let you do the things you want to do in your life. Sometimes fear hinders your progress and lets you down before you begin the first step of your journey to success. But what is worry or fear?

These are both states of mind which humans easily create. The main cause of worry is ignorance. When you worry about little things in your life all the time, they start coming true. Then you wonder why all these bad things happen. The law of attraction states that whatever you think about will come to you, and whatever you resist, persists. I used to worry about everything from the time I was very young. Due to all my worry and negative thinking habits, I always missed out on the good things I wanted to enjoy. I always imagined the worst.

This is a cause of unnecessary stress. Beyond your fears lives your dream life. Since I started doing my positive thinking habits and small disciplines on a day-to-day basis, everything started falling into place. My worry habits changed into positive, uplifting habits which are moving me forward and closer to my goals. I mainly got rid of worry by understanding the things I was worried about. As the main cause of worry is ignorance, once you start understanding the problem by doing more research, it will fade away in seconds. Worry can only be overcome by studying the things you are worried about, because when you study, you develop faith. Faith is a simple state of mind induced by repeated, positive self-talk. I started speaking positively from the moment I got up in the morning until I retired for the day. Once you start developing more and more faith in yourself and your goals, you start living happily. Each small goal you achieve builds your faith.

Before this, I owned a veterinary hospital. I was working very hard, but hardly making ends meet. I couldn't understand why it wasn't happening, why I wasn't successful. I worked very hard for six years at that hospital with little success, always short of money. When I saw other veterinarians who were doing well and making lots of money, I thought that maybe my location wasn't as good or my hospital wasn't as good as theirs. I was wrong. During that time, I worked and did nothing else. I hardly read any positive thinking or self-help books, and never attended any seminars. I thought that you could only make money by working hard at your job. Even when I had one hospital, I was trying to buy another hospital with my limited funds. I was under the impression that having another hospital would help my finances. However, if your one kid is not doing well, having more kids is not going to help. I struggled and struggled while working hard. During those six years, I never took any vacation. I didn't want to miss a single day's pay. Even at home and on weekends, I was wondering about my practice and what I should do. I didn't see light coming from anywhere.

Then I moved to California and started working a federal job. I still wanted to know how to become successful as a veterinarian. I still had the same philosophy and attitude, but no improvement. I was doing the same things, but expecting different results. This is called insanity. Then I came across some great motivational speaker lectures. One of these, Jim Rohn, a great philosopher, changed my life forever. I learned philosophy, discipline, habits, personal growth, and to have a great attitude by listening to his recorded seminars. Jim Rohn influenced me so much. I started studying all his books and listened to him constantly. You can find his great recorded seminars on YouTube. I made a habit of listening to him for 15 minutes every day. This simple habit brought improvements in my financial world, as well as personally and professionally. I've continued listening to him because it dramatically changed every aspect of my life. I am still so inspired by his thoughts, his philosophies, and his way of motivating and inspiring people. He has left us, God bless his soul. One of the best things he shared in his books and imprinted in my mind, which totally blew my mind, is this statement:

> "When you work hard at your job, you make a living.
> When you work hard on yourself, you make a fortune."

I thought and said to myself, "Wow! What a great philosophy to motivate and inspire people to succeed." You already know it worked for me. I am still doing it since learning it from him.

Since I started working on myself and my habits, everything started improving for me. All my goals were being met.

I started attracting people who helped me achieve them. This simple step of working on myself made a huge and dramatic impact on my life. I was wondering, *IS THIS REALLY TRUE? How are all these beautiful things coming into my life?*

Sometimes it was hard to believe how easily things were coming to me: happiness, wealth, good health and great social groups. I couldn't believe the difference between struggling so hard at my job and how easy it was now. This all happened due to some simple self-improvement steps I took and still take. Do this and your life will never be the same. You'll need a telescope to find your old, pre-self-improvement self. Actually, even if you had one, you couldn't find your old self. When I look back now, I'm a completely different person than I was – in the best way possible!

Here's what I did every day:

– Read self-help books for at least 30 minutes, no matter where I was. Even if I was traveling, I didn't miss reading. I'd miss a meal before my reading. I enjoy reading self-help books and look forward to it. I set up a specific time during the day for reading. It's easy to find 30 minutes during the day or in the evening to read. It's had a big impact in changing the person I am today.

– Listened to audio self-help books. My drive to work is about 20 minutes. During that time, I listen to self-help audio books. If you listen for 30 minutes a day, by the end of the year, you've easily completed a degree in self-help or motivational knowledge. I buy one self-help audio book per month, and during that month, I listen to that audio for the entire month. This gives me a very good handle on this new audio, and it gets embedded in my mind. Repetition is very important when you want to learn a new skill. Repetition is the mother of skill. Don't miss the opportunity to learn during your commute. Your drive is the best learning time since nobody can bother you. You're completely immersed in your self-help world of books while enjoying your drive. Don't waste this opportunity to learn during your drive time. Use your drive time wisely. This also sets the tone of your beautiful day in the morning. It's a continuation of doing the self-appreciation exercise in the mirror. It keeps those good vibes going. When you listen to self-help books in the morning, you'll feel good and uplifted. Feeling good is the main thing that makes your dreams come true. Your subconscious mind works according to your feelings and makes it real. When you feel good, you can't think bad thoughts. When you feel bad, you can't think good thoughts. When you feel good, you are stopping the flow of what you don't want in your life. When you feel good, you're attracting all the goals you want to flow continuously to you. Even when you feel good for only a few seconds, during that time, you're attracting everything you want and repelling everything you don't want.

Here's more of what I did daily, which helped me achieve my goals and become a millionaire:

- Said my gratitude prayer in the morning. You can create your own prayer. For example: "I am grateful that today I am feeling happy, healthy, wealthy, and prosperous, and I'm enjoying my life."

- Visualized everything I wanted in my life. (I'll discuss visualization in the following chapter. It's one of the most important rituals I do every day. It made a huge impact in shaping my millionaire life).

Don't wait for the perfect moment to change yourself. The time is right now and here. All you have is now. Don't think about the past or your failures. Just enjoy this moment. Whatever you do in this moment has the potential to bring health, wealth, contentment, prosperity and joy to your life, so act accordingly. Don't worry about anything. By worrying, you won't end up anywhere but in a dark cloud of doubt, anxiety and depression. Kick worry out of your life by listening to self-help audio books, using positive self-talk and reading every day. You'll never regret starting these new uplifting and empowering habits. Your world will be full of good things. If I can do it, so can you. Nobody but you is stopping you from the life you want to live. Be the person you want to be right now. Don't waste another moment. Time is priceless. You can get anything in life except for more time. Everybody is assigned twenty-four hours in a day. Start seeing your dreams until they come true. Dream until your dreams come true!

CHAPTER NINE

Mind Images Empower Your Life

"Mind images are the telescope through which you can plan your life and achieve whatever you see through those images."

– Dr. Mann

Looking at the heading of this chapter, you might be wondering what mind images are and how they empower your life. Mind images helped to bring me success, love, money, good health and everything I wanted in my life. I'll explain how. It definitely works and will definitely, without fail, bring all the things you want in your life. This is one of the best lessons I've learned. I was totally ignorant about how the mind works. I learned this lesson from Bob Proctor. He explained that our minds think in images. For instance, if you think about your house, you'll see an image of your house in your mind's eye. If you think about your car, an image of your car comes into your mind. Mind images are what we see on the screen of our mind all day long. Mind images are the images we see on the screen of our subconscious mind. Everybody has the ability to see mind images. If you're thinking about a past memory, like when you bought your first bicycle when you were a kid, a picture of your bicycle comes to mind. You can tell me exactly what color it was and how it looked. That's what I mean by "mind image."

Everyone has mind images. Our minds are powerful, and one of the best machines in the world. Most people aren't aware of the mind's power and what it can do for us. Whatever mind images we see, whether these things happened in our life or we're just thinking about them, they have a huge impact on our day-to-day life. The only difference between successful and unsuccessful people is that successful people know how to use their mind effectively in their daily life. It's not hard to do. I've told you how easy it is. In reality, we do this every day, but aren't aware of it. However, we can become aware of the images we see and choose only the images we want to create in our life. When we do this, life becomes a phenomenal and wonderful ride – just the way we want it to be! A ritual you can use on a daily basis is to think about all the good things you want in your life. If you are wondering how thinking is related to mind images, thinking brings images to your mind. Our minds don't think in words; they think in pictures. Again, suppose I told you to think about what kind of car you drive. A clear and precise picture of your car would come to your mind. That's what I mean. Whenever we think, we see pictures and images of what we're thinking about. When you think about good things, good things follow you and flow into your life. When you think about negative or destructive things, these follow in the same way. The law of attraction brings what you think about into your life. It's that simple, and due to its simplicity, people don't believe it. The world is complicated, so we think there must be some complicated, difficult system for success in life. But in reality, success is simple. It's a matter of following easy habits daily and consistently. It's the daily habits that bring you everything you want. If you want good health and you start eating an apple a day, you'll achieve good health. Walking every day keeps you in good shape. Remember that famous quote, "An apple a day keeps the doctor away?" It's simple to do and brings the results you want. At the same time, though, it's easy not to do.

When you think about any incident (good or bad) that happened in your life, it will affect your future big time. If that incident is good and inspiring, it will bring good things by changing the frequency of vibration. You'll feel good simply by thinking about that incident. If you're in these feel-good vibrations and thinking about something you want, your mind will bring it to you since your subconscious mind doesn't know the difference between real and imagined. Initially, I was hesitant about this and didn't believe I could manifest things just by thinking and seeing the images in my mind's eye with full conviction and belief. Then an incident happened. I'd like to share that incident with you. Maybe it will help you to believe in what I'm talking about.

When I was reading and learning about how mind images can help me achieve my goals, I set a goal to travel to India in business class. I'd never traveled business class before. The reason I hadn't is because the ticket costs about 10 times more than economy class. I had no idea what international business class seats or international traveling looked like. I hadn't experienced it before, so it was hard for me to see mental images of business class. I searched the internet and downloaded business class seating and its comfort and made it my screensaver. I started seeing it every day in my mind and I felt what it would be like to travel in that comfortable environment. I was going to India in three months and bought an economy class ticket, but I continued my exercise of seeing the mind images and feeling the emotions. I was flying from LA to Frankfurt, and then to Delhi. I flew to Frankfurt in economy class. When boarding the plane from Frankfurt to Delhi, the air hostess asked me to step aside. To tell you the truth, I got scared that they'd found something in my bag that wasn't supposed to be there. If you've traveled via plane, you know about all the security regulations for our well-being and safety. I'm grateful to all airlines for doing that. I waited there, thinking about all the things that could have gone wrong – you know, that's how our minds work.

Finally, about 15 minutes later, the air hostess said, "Sir, we're so sorry. We gave your seat to a family because they wanted to sit close together. Would you mind traveling in business class?"

"Oh, yes, I don't mind at all," I told her. I was so happy and so grateful for this validation of my work with mind images. Not only did I get to travel in business class, but now I truly believed in this beautiful and powerful mind work. It not only gave me the comfort of traveling in business class, but it totally put my life on a beautiful journey to success. Since then, I've never looked back and never ever doubted this mind image philosophy. It's beautiful, and it's kind of a secret that I found. I've used this secret for my well-being, good health, abundance and my beautiful, loving family life. I have SO much gratitude for finding this beautiful secret.

I said 'beautiful' for a reason. This secret allowed me to find so much inner beauty in my life. This is hidden in every one of us. Everybody is born rich and awesome in life. You have to find the inner genius within you that is sleeping. My life be-came more and more beautiful, abundant and wealthy by doing these simple, workable techniques. I call it a secret because so many people don't know about it. And even if they do know it, they never use it.

Ralph Waldo Emerson says,

"we become what we think about all day long."

Think about good things all the time. Think about them all day long, and you'll never lack anything – not happiness, health, wealth, prosperity or success. Try it! You won't regret it. Think about the way you want your life to be. Only you can decide and think about your life; no one else can do this for you. The only person who can create the life of your dreams is YOU. Who can create and think about your dream life? Yes, you guessed right: YOU.

As Jim Rohn mentioned all the time in his inspiring and life-changing seminars:

"The major key to your better future is YOU."

The most powerful, easiest thing you can do is to see images on the screen of your mind for at least 15 minutes every day. Find a time during the day and go to a quiet, comfortable place in your house or office. Then close your eyes and see the images as you are living them. The images can be good health, your beautiful, loving relationship, your dream job, a life of luxury, and all the things you'd like to have in your life that please you and empower you. Mind images are the secret of my life, and you can make it your secret too. If you do, you'll never face lack in your life.

Here I'd like to mention a great quote by a great man who used a mental image to shape history by putting a seed of independence in the minds of millions of Indian people. They followed him relentlessly because they believed in him.

Mahatma Gandhi, in my opinion, was a great example of how to use mind power. He used this power to make history.

**"A man is but the product of his thoughts.
What he thinks, he becomes."**

– Mahatma Gandhi

CHAPTER TEN

Self-perception is the Key to An Abundant Millionaire Life

In this chapter, I'll discuss how self-image and self-knowledge helped me become a millionaire and a better human being. If you become a better human being, money won't be an issue. Money will follow you if you do more for other people. Initially, even when I became a veterinarian, I had a low self-image. I always considered myself less than the professionals around me. I thought the other professionals were better than me. I was under the impression that if I were a medical doctor or a dentist or engineer, I would've been very successful and wealthy. I always thought my colleagues were making more money than me and happier in their lives. I was under the impression that other professions had more scope for advancement or better opportunities to make more money and become successful. Since I graduated from veterinary school, I thought this field was very under-paid. While this was my mindset, I didn't meet any veterinarians who were very successful. I still had low self-esteem. I was just making ends meet, as I mentioned earlier – even with long hours and no time off. I was definitely lacking money. If I had to travel anywhere, I had to think about it long and hard, because where was the money going to come from? Even if I took a vacation for a few days, I was always thinking about my hospital and practice. I felt I should have one more practice for more advancement in my life. This lasted for the next seven or eight years. I was doing my regular work and thinking about how I could do better and make more money.

Then my wife introduced me to self-help books. The first book I read was *Notes from a Friend* by Anthony Robbins. I still read that book on and off. It didn't do much for me at the time because I was still stuck in scarcity thinking. That book did help me pass my board exams, but I didn't follow it until later. I wasn't consistent in reading and listening to self-help books and audio. Outwardly, I was reading books constantly, but inside, my self-image was still low and didn't change. I didn't know enough to change my self-image. I didn't know I needed to change my life by working harder on myself than on my job. Then one day while I was working out in the gym, I came across lectures from Jim Rohn on YouTube. His lectures totally changed my perception about myself and my life. He was talking about his life and how he was a failure, and then became a millionaire and a success. He mentioned that he was not very educated, but still managed to become successful. He said if he can do it, anybody can. In his book, he mentioned his philosophy on life, which is very important. This one quote of his changed my whole life. I never looked back, and everything just fell into place. He said, and kept repeating:

> **"If you work hard at your job, you can make a living.**
> **If you work hard on yourself, you can make a fortune."**

> – Jim Rohn

When I was listening to him, I thought and felt that he was talking to me directly. I never met him in person. I just listened to his lectures and his great wisdom, as he had already passed away. I'm so grateful to him for making me who I am today. All my life, I'll remain grateful to him for guiding me and inspiring me. I introduced and implemented his philosophy on life into my life. Initially, I thought that by working hard, you become successful, but it's actually when you start working hard on yourself that you become a wonderful human being, and become successful. Your perception about yourself changes when you're continuously working on yourself. By learning about how your mind works, how your life works, and how all these universal laws work, you feel energized. You feel good about yourself, and your self-image just automatically changes. When your self-images changes, your perception of yourself changes. This all leads to your vibrational alignment. You become more aligned with the higher power, and once you get aligned with the higher power, you aren't deficient in anything you want. The higher power is the infinite supply; from here, you can get whatever you want.

Making a commitment to read self-help books for 30 minutes every day for a year changed my entire life. My knowledge about the mind changed, and most importantly, my philosophy of life changed. By simply reading self-help books and listening to audio books every day, everything from my health to my bank balance changed. Jim Rohn was right: by working hard on yourself, you can make a fortune. I'll always follow this simple practice of reading and listening to self-help and mind-empowering books. Every day, whatever you do, make a difference. If you do bad things every day, it will make your life miserable. Instead, practice positive, inspiring and empowering habits to make your life beautiful, wonderful and abundant in all aspects. It will guide you to make a fortune instead of living a mediocre life.

I know some of you have low self-esteem, but please stop thinking that way about yourself. You are God's highest creation, and you have creative power like God. You are unique and have a mind which is one of the most powerful tools in the world. This is easy to see when you look at all the great things invented by humans. They were initially an idea in the mind of someone before they appeared in reality. Don't think you aren't great like the Wright brothers or Edison or Bell; you have everything you need to live a successful and abundant life.

Self-image is the key to living a successful life. If I can do this through these simple practices of working hard on myself, you can do it too. There's nothing impossible in this life. Make the commitment to start working on yourself today instead of working hard on your job. If you really want to live the life that your heart desires, don't wait another day or another month or another year. Life is too short to focus on the negatives. Start reading every day for 30 minutes. It's a simple discipline, but I'm positive that it will do magic for you and make all your dreams come true. Don't waste a single moment. Get ready for this beautiful life! Life has wonders to offer; be ready to receive. God, your higher power, or your inner world, wants you to be successful, wealthy, healthy, harmonious and happy. He wants you to be rich and have every luxury of life that you imagined for yourself – every dream that you're dreaming, every opportunity you're waiting for. Think highly of yourself. You're the highest creation of God with God's powers. Start behaving the way you want to be. Self-image is the first and most important step in preparation for a successful life.

George Bernard Shaw says:

"Progress is impossible without change, and those who cannot change their minds cannot change anything."

CHAPTER ELEVEN

Serenity is the Door to the Treasure House of Wealth, Wisdom, Happiness and Health

A small habit that helped me to get a handle on the beauty of this abundant life is serenity of mind. In our daily life, we're so busy with all the chores related to family, work and entertainment, that we don't have time to even think about what we really want. To find out what we really want, we have to think about our dreams and things in life that we actually want. Most people just wander, without ever finding out their real goal or real passion in life. You could say they just wander through life without actually achieving or getting or becoming what their passion is and without knowing why they're here or what their purpose in life is. Whenever I go to any meeting or social gathering, I like to talk to as many people as I can. My first question is usually, "What's your goal? What do you really want to do in your life?" People look at me and try to figure out what I mean. They tell me that what we want doesn't matter, that the main thing is what we are worthy of and what we're getting. They say wanting has nothing to do with their necessities. Overall, they don't answer my question. In reality, it's not their fault, because they are unaware of this beautiful secret of life. You can get whatever you want from life. Life can offer you everything if you're clear about what you want and ask life for it.

I was also in that same category before I started reading and doing research about success in life, and why some people are successful and others aren't. After reading self-help books, listening to audio books and attending seminars, I came to know and understand how the mind works. One of the best exercises I learned is from the book *The Power of Positive Thinking* by Dr. Norman Vincent Peale. It helped me decide what I really wanted in life by focusing on my inner wants and what really matters to me. I used the silence exercise for this. Initially, I wasn't very impressed, and my mind wandered here and there, but after a few days it started calming down and I really felt the inner connection that I never realized existed inside me. Some people call this the inner voice, inner man or silent partner. This feeling of realization and becoming aware of this beautiful world opened the gate to abundance, prosperity, happiness, joy and peace. This simple exercise helped me so much that it's hard sometimes to put into words what it did for me. I call this exercise "the beauty of silence." Silence makes you feel what you've never felt before, and see the things you've never realized or seen before. It makes you feel serene and peaceful. When you are in that state, your mind does wonders for you and opens a world of abundance in all aspects of life. The mind is so powerful that after a period of silence, it gives you so many ideas. Sometimes a solution comes to you for a previous problem when you are not even thinking about that problem! As James Allen says in his wonderful book, *As a Man Thinketh*:

"Calmness of mind is one of the most beautiful jewels of wisdom. It is the result of long and patient effort in self-control. Its presence is an indication of ripened experience, and of a more than ordinary knowledge of the laws and operations of thought."

He's right. Whenever we're calm and peaceful, infinite power flows freely and easily through us. When we're at ease with the world, our mind works better and we come up with brilliant ideas all the time. To live a wonderful life, you need only one idea that changes your life forever. I've been doing this silence exercise since I read about it in that marvelous book. I've implemented it into my life and it became a phenomenal ride to abundance, prosperity, joy, happiness and wealth.

The silence exercise goes like this:

Every day for about 15 minutes, go to a quiet room and be silent. Don't read or write. Just sit or lie down.

Initially, I wondered how this exercise had anything to do with my life. But then I thought, let me give it a try. For the first few days, I was just quiet during that time. A bunch of thoughts came to mind, or I was thinking about all the issues of the day. As I continued this exercise for few more days, it totally blew my mind. After the silence exercise, I felt energized and refreshed. My mind was actually more vibrant and vivid. When your mind is clear, beautiful thoughts start coming to you.

After that exercise my mind told me to write, so I started writing after the silence exercise for seven minutes. I do this every day, and now I look forward to the silence. All the good ideas that came to mind, I implemented in my business, which created a lot of wealth. More than anything, though, it makes me feel serene, steadfast and successful. If I have any issues during the day, or any kind of hard tasks, I present them to my mind after practicing the silence exercise. Sometimes the solution immediately comes to my mind, and sometimes it will pop into my mind when I'm not thinking about it at all – but it always comes sooner or later. For instance, I wasn't sure what I should call my website. I thought long and hard but no ideas came, or I didn't like the ones that did. After the silence exercise, beautiful and great ideas came. Silence opens the door to a treasure house, and from there you can get anything you want. The silence exercise will not only make you successful; it will also make you serene and calm.

When you're calm, people enjoy your company, and they can learn from you and rely on you. When you're calm, you're in vibrational alignment with the higher power who can give you everything. Calmness helps you achieve your dreams and fulfill your desires. Silence is that beautiful state of mind when all abundant ideas flood in. You can find the solution to any problem when you're connected to the higher power. Silence is a pure gem of life. Implement silence in your life to be happy, abundant, harmonious, healthy and wealthy. Don't wait for the perfect moment to start this exercise. Do it now. This exercise was mind-blowing for me since it helped me achieve my goals and get some wonderful ideas that I implemented in my life. My life became a successful, happy journey.

Initially, you can try the silence exercise for three minutes every day. Then, every week, start increasing that by two minutes until you reach 15 minutes. You can do this exercise whenever your schedule allows – in the morning, evening, or before retiring for the day. I do mine in the evening, because at that time, I'm free and relaxed after taking a shower. I go to my quiet place and do the exercise. Once you incorporate this habit into your life, you won't be lacking in anything. I believe you'll be healthier, happier and wealthier. This simple exercise can make your dreams come true. Fill your life with abundance in all aspects by being silent for 15 minutes. I start my silence exercise with the serenity prayer:

> *"God, grant me the serenity to accept the things*
> *I cannot change, the courage to change the things I can,*
> *and the wisdom to know the difference."*

Silence is the real tonic for mind and body. I'm going to end these beautiful thoughts on this great mind-enriching exercise with these words of wisdom from my favorite actor, Mel Gibson:

> *"The thing we're all looking for is happiness, and if*
> *we achieve just a modicum of that, or even a little piece*
> *of serenity, even for five minutes a day, we're lucky."*

By becoming serene, you'll be more successful, calmer, and more energized. Let silence open the floodgates of infinite intelligence in your wonderful life.

CHAPTER TWELVE

A Glorious Millionaire Life is the Result of Feeling Great All Day Long

This is also one of the habits or simple daily exercises that helped me achieve my goals in life. I didn't know what to do when I set goals, or how to think positive all the time. All the books and audios I listened to always focused on staying positive and thinking positive, but I didn't get it. My question to everybody, and to myself was, "How can I think positive if I'm lacking money and late paying bills? Oh yeah, and my business isn't going well either." I didn't see my dreams being fulfilled. Everything around me was falling apart. I didn't have any money and I didn't see any money coming to me. How could I stay positive? That was my biggest challenge. HOW?

I was always looking for an answer to this great question. I knew I needed to find the answer to the question of how to stay positive when it feels like I'm in the center of an obstacle hurricane. They say that if you're looking for something, you'll surely find it. The *Bible* tells us, "Ask, and it shall be given unto you." At last, I found the answer while I was reading a self-help book by Ralph Waldo Emerson. It's a simple quote, but it's really powerful if you pay attention to every word. He says, "We become what we think about all day long." After reading that quote, my mind went *WHOO! That's what makes you positive all the time, and what makes you think positive, too!* If a person becomes what he thinks about all day long, you need to think positive thoughts all day long. In order to think positive, you have to surround yourself with positive- minded people or read positive, inspiring, uplifting books and listen to great motivational talks.

This is stuff you can easily find on the internet. You don't have to look anywhere; great material is available at no cost. Any kind of book you can find at your local library is free of cost. All my life, I only read books related to my studies and never read any self-help books. I thought reading books related to my field and working hard in my job would make me wealthy and prosperous. Since I started reading or listening to positive self-help books and attending seminars, my thinking started changing automatically. I don't have to work hard to think positive anymore, because reading all that material made me think like a successful person. When my thinking started changing, my life started changing. My mind became more conditioned to abundance in all aspects of life, and I became "success conscious." It's true: my life simply changed by changing my thoughts. Every day, all day long, I thought about this great motivational reading I was putting into my subconscious mind. I changed my mental diet from negative thinking to positive, which did wonders for me.

You know, your mind is the ruler of the world. If you can control your mind, you can control your life. You can become what you want to become by putting good stuff into your mind. It's these simple daily habits which will turn your life around in no time. You'll be astonished to see the results in your life. You'll wonder why everything started showing up in your life, just like I did. I read and focused on my books when I woke up in the morning. Instead of watching TV or spending time with negative people around me, I set up daily time to listen to all this positive stuff. Once I got into reading and listening, I began spending more and more time with people who were experienced in this field. At the time, I didn't know anybody who was motivational and inspiring and doing this kind of positive thinking, but you don't have to know the person personally to start getting results. I hadn't met any of the motivational speakers, but I knew what they did on a daily basis to make a difference in their lives. Now you can get all their wonderful knowledge on the internet and YouTube. You can watch all of their previously recorded messages, which I was doing and still do every day. Certain habits I was repeating every day were giving me results that built my confidence more and more. I was seeing changes in my life big time. Why should I stop doing that? No way! I'll continue all these simple, effective things which I'm recommending you follow. I know and have experienced how these simple rituals make a huge difference.

I can give you another example. I wanted to buy a house, and read in one of the books about visualization – that you have to think about the thing you want to bring into your life. You have to feel the emotion that you'll feel when you have the house now, before you acquire it. I tried and tried. Nothing happened for a month. I had a picture of the house on my laptop as my screensaver. After a month, my realtor called and said, "I think I have the house you're looking for." My wife and I went to see the house. As soon as we entered the house, I felt the feeling I was feeling when I visualized the house every day. I felt like I'd been here before, and actually, I had been to the house in my visualization many times. Whatever you can think about and feel good about, you will definitely see in reality; this is the law. Since I came to know this secret of life, I use it every day and am enjoying my life to the fullest. This is the secret of manifesting a glorious millionaire lifestyle. You must think all the time about the life you want to live, the money you want to have, and the happiness and health you desire. All your thoughts become reality. Whatever you thought about when you were young, you're living that life now. Whatever you are going to think, you will live that life – so think big. Think about the beautiful, abundant, happy, healthy and wonderful life you want to live. You are the master of your thoughts and the captain of your soul. You are the creator of your destiny. You can do whatever you want in your life, because only you can think of what you want. Nobody can do it for you. Life is waiting, and you can achieve that beautiful, wonderful life by thinking about it with the strong belief that you are going to get it. Belief in the thing you want is the turning point in achieving it.

Life unfolds however you want. If you're not thinking big or about abundance, your mind has a tendency to think about scarcity. Guess what? If you're thinking about scarcity, then that's what you'll bring into your life. It's your choice how you want to condition your mind. If you want success in your life, you have to be success-conscious by thinking and reading about success. If you want more money, you have to make your mind money-conscious. It's your choice whether you experience lack or abundance; it's your thinking that makes the change in your life. You'll become what you think about, so why not think beautiful, wonderful, good, happy and positive thoughts? I changed my life from one of lack to abundance with daily rituals that helped me to think BIG. I read positive self-help books and kept the company of great, successful people (that you can access on the internet) by attending seminars of great motivational speakers and reading their books. You can get all the books from a library. Knowledge is everywhere, but it's up to you to access it. There's no lack of resources to help you achieve whatever you want in life. Don't wait a day, an hour or a month. Start doing it right now. You can get whatever you want; you just have to know what you really want. Life has everything to give. Just do these disciplines every day. Your dreams and an abundant life is waiting for you. Simply change your thinking and the results will be phenomenal – but you have to think every day. Research says that only three percent of people think they are successful. Thinking is also a ritual, and you have to sit down and focus every day on what you want to bring into your life and how you want to live your life. You have to do the work to live the life you want. There's no such thing as something for nothing. On the subject of achieving success, the great motivational speaker Jim Rohn says:

"Success is neither magical nor mysterious.
Success is the natural consequence of consistently applying
the basic fundamentals."

Start living your dreams and create a successful life by becoming the person you want to be.

CHAPTER THIRTEEN

Becoming A Millionaire by Keeping Part of Your Money

*"Here's the philosophy of the rich and the poor.
Poor people spend their money and invest what's left.
The rich invest their money and spend what's left."*

– Jim Rohn

In order to become a millionaire, what's important is not how much you earn, but how much you keep. That's the secret to becoming a millionaire. I'm going to tell you about the simple techniques that worked for me and made me huge amounts of money. Most people pay their bills first and keep whatever's left to save, invest or have fun with. Most people don't have any money left after paying their bills and household expenses. If you tell them they have to save, they'll say, "This month we're short, so we don't have anything to save." They say they'll start tomorrow, and their tomorrow never comes. The law of freedom and financial success says you have to save at least 10 percent of what you earn. This law has worked for me since I came to know this wonderful magic formula. I made a commitment to save at least 10 percent of the money I earned. Since I started following this simple formula, I never have to look for money. Instead, money is following me. Whatever money I need for an investment or to buy a house with is there. When I look at my bank account, I find more than I expect. It's there whenever I need it.

Before finding out about this formula for financial freedom, I was like most people. I was under the impression that you can only become a millionaire or become financially independent by making millions of dollars. Then I realized that to some extent, that's true – but if you're not saving any of your millions, you can still go broke and not have any money left.

Once, my CPA came to my office at the end of the year to discuss the taxes for the year. She was very impressed with how I handled my money and planning. She told me I was very organized. She mentioned that one of her clients was making four million dollars a year, but when she went to his office to discuss his taxes, she was astonished that he didn't have any money set aside to pay taxes. She said, "What do you mean? You're earning four million a year!" He told her he'd spent it all. So, it's not how much you make; it's what you do with that money. I simply followed the formula and always have money, because I'm always saving 10 percent of what I earn.

When you have money, you become confident and don't worry about bills. Indirectly, you're conditioning your mind to trust money. Your mind starts thinking it's easy to make money, and you become money-conscious. Money is just a state of mind. When your mind gets conditioned to money, you won't have any scarcity. Unfortunately, though, most people who are struggling financially are stuck in poverty and scarcity. If you're thinking of poverty, it won't bring you any money, just like flooding your mind with worry and fear won't allow you to enjoy anything in life. Fear and worry block the flow of abundance to your life. Becoming a millionaire or financially free isn't about working hard; it's simply about conditioning your mind to money. If you want to be happy, you have to condition your mind to happiness. If you are success-conscious, you'll become successful. Saving part of your money for yourself will condition your mind to money, and you'll never be deprived. Start today. Put aside ten percent of the money you earn. I did this by making ten percent automatically go to my savings account. That way, you won't see the money coming out of your checking account. If you aren't doing it automatically, some months you won't do it. You'll start thinking that you had more expenses this month, and tell yourself you'll do it next month. Just set up an automatic transfer. You won't believe how, in a short period of time, you'll have money you never imagined having. If you want to become a millionaire or you want financial freedom, definitely start this practice today. You can't imagine how much relief you'll feel when you are no longer anxious from the stress of money scarcity. Have you ever heard of lottery winners who are broke a year after winning big? Why is that? It's because when they won the lottery and got a huge amount of money, their mind wasn't conditioned to money, so they lost it or spent it all after a short time.

How do you condition your mind to money? I followed a simple practice I heard in a Tony Robbins lecture. Day by day, it conditions your mind for money. A few months ago, I started keeping $300-$400 dollars cash in my wallet. This gave me confidence that I have money whenever I need it. If I have to buy something, I can, as I have the money. If I go to the mall and like a certain thing, I don't have to think twice about buying it. Prior to this, if I was at the mall and liked something, I'd always think it was too expensive. In reality, it wasn't too expensive; my mind was just in scarcity mode. Since I started doing this cash practice, my mind has become conditioned to money. I always have money in my wallet and I always have money flowing in and out of my life. My wealth is multiplying every day, simply by doing this practice.

One day, I was talking to a friend who lives in another state. We were talking about money, and he mentioned he was lacking money. He runs his own business and works very hard working long hours, and he's still struggling with money and just making ends meet. I shared my money consciousness strategies with him and he started doing them. Three or four weeks later, he called me and said thank you. I asked him why he was thanking me. He said, "For bringing money and wealth into my life." He told me that since we'd last spoken, he'd tried my method of keeping money in his wallet. He also began saying these wealth affirmations:

"My wealth multiplies every day."

"I love money and money is good."

"I am so happy and grateful that money comes to me continuously on a consistent basis."

He told me he's now flooded with new clients. "It's working magic in my life," he told me. "For the last two or three weeks, I've been really busy in my business."

What are you thinking about? If you're reading this book, you're also lacking money in your life. Don't worry – it's never too late. Start today, and I can assure you that you'll be on the path to abundance. One day you'll thank me for sharing this simple strategy for earning more money. Start implementing this simple ritual in your life and money will flow to you because you'll become money-conscious. Saving money is a habit. Adopt this habit today. If you can't save money on what you earn today, you will never be able to save in the future. Don't wait. Start the wheel of fortune spinning in your life today. You have nothing to lose, but a life to win.

CHAPTER FOURTEEN

Giving Away Money Opens the Door to More Wealth

"I never would have been able to tithe the first million dollars I ever made if I had not tithed my first salary, which was $1.50 per week."

– John D. Rockefeller

It's true that giving away money opens the door to great and abundant wealth. I always thought I couldn't give money because I didn't have enough. Maybe that's why I didn't have much. I was always thinking about lack and telling everyone the same story: "I'm lacking money. I don't make enough and I'm just making ends meet." I remember how hard I worked, but somehow I never had much to give or to spend. Anytime someone needy asked me for help, I told them I didn't have any money to spare. I told them that after paying all my expenses, I had nothing left – and I was telling the truth! I was working hard, but always thinking about scarcity and lack, which is why I was always lacking money and hardly had any money left all the time. It didn't matter whether I was working one job or two jobs. I was always looking for ways to increase my income without conditioning my mind to money. I was ignorant about money consciousness, and I know most people are like me. They don't know about wealth-building techniques, or how powerful the mind is. It's not their fault that they lack money. These things aren't taught in school.

When I was struggling with money, lack showed up in my life everywhere. I thought about giving only when I had some extra money, which was almost never. I was under the impression that you can make money only by working hard. I also thought that I could only give money if I was making a lot of money. That's not true. I finally realized I could make more money by giving part of what I earned to some good, charitable causes. According to the law of giving and receiving, whenever you give money, you've started the receiving process. You're definitely going to get more than you give as long as you're giving from the heart. I'm not saying you don't have to work hard – but at the same time, you have to work smart.

Since I changed my approach to getting rich and becoming a millionaire, I have abundance in my life and always have enough to take care of my needs, my family's needs and any luxuries we'd like. I studied the most successful people and how they came to have all the money they want to enjoy every luxury you can think of. This technique of tithing is a simple approach to living your dream life and owning everything you want. It's simply giving part of your money to great causes that help those in need.

If you are struggling to make money and you think you can't give away any funds because you don't have enough to fulfill your basic needs, your mind is conditioned to lack and scarcity. To gain abundance, you have to give part of your money to charities and those less fortunate than you. You have to believe that you have enough to give away. In this way, you put the law of giving and receiving into action. Universal laws never fail. They always work; they have to. It's the law, right? The process of giving opens the door to abundance, wealth and prosperity. When you start giving, the receiving process begins immediately. This is the law. Whatever you give comes back to you multiplied. It's a cycle. It's how the universe operates. Since I started giving, money flows freely into my life. Initially, I didn't know what happened, but after studying the tithing process, I understand how it works. It also feels good when you help people or serve great causes. Whatever you can contribute makes you feel great on the inside. You feel a sense of satisfaction. Be sure to always give from the heart. I usually give 5 percent of what I earn and it always comes back to me. Giving truly opens the door to greater wealth and makes you feel real satisfaction, which is priceless. Give whatever you can to charity or church or any institution that works for a good cause. There are an enormous number of institutions that do a great job by providing health services, food and medical care to those less fortunate. You can get all this information from the internet. Please make it a habit to donate whatever you can. Once you acquire this habit, you'll always be blessed with great wealth, good health and a wonderful life. You'll always be happy and satisfied when you give either your money or your time.

Here's one simple affirmation I repeat every day about tithing. It has worked miracles for me, and it can do the same for you:

> *"I am a great philanthropist who donates money*
> *to institutions that serve humanity."*

Make tithing your habit and you'll have abundance in all aspects of your life. The secret to living a great and self-fulfilled life is giving part of your earnings to charities, or to those in need. Once you have adopted this philosophy and embedded this lesson in your mind, your life will become fulfilling beyond your anticipation. Start with very small amounts. It will work like a miracle in your life.

CHAPTER FIFTEEN

Meditation Brings Wisdom and Wealth

*"Prayer is when you talk to god.
Meditation is when god talks to you."*

– Unknown

Meditation is a beautiful, serene practice that helps you calm your mind and opens the door to great wealth and prosperity. Wealth doesn't always mean money; it means abundance in all aspects of life. People think meditation is very complicated and serious. They can't keep their minds from wandering for very long. Any new skill you acquire needs practice. Practice makes you perfect in any field. It's the same as learning to ride a bicycle when you're young or learning to play a new instrument, or even writing simple English – they all require practice. Everything in life takes practice. Any skill needs practice.

In order to gain something, you have to give something. Giving doesn't always mean giving money or making great sacrifices, though. You can't have something for nothing. It's a universal law. You have to pay the price. In order to become a millionaire, you have to do simple practices every day. You have to make them a daily habit, whether you feel like it or not.

When I started meditation, I didn't know much about it. One day, I just made up my mind to start this wonderful practice. I started by simply closing my eyes, focusing on the middle of my eyes, and thinking about some positive and empowering experience from the past. That's how I started doing meditation. Meditation simply makes you feel quiet and relaxed for some time, depending on how much time you want to invest in this practice. Also, people are under the wrong impression that you have to meditate for hours in order to see results. I only meditate for seven minutes every day, and it works like magic for me. It makes me more serene, calm, focused and attentive. When you're more attentive, you're more productive at work. Whatever you do, meditation will make you more successful. I also find that it makes me more open to my internal guidance; answers to whatever questions I have come to me during or after meditation.

When you meditate, your mind becomes really calm and composed. During that time, when you visualize something, it goes directly to your subconscious mind. Whatever you can think in your mind, you can get in reality. When I wanted to become a millionaire, that's what I thought about after my meditation. After meditating for seven minutes, I'd visualize money flowing freely into my life, and my business flourishing. I'd think about it and see that in my mind before going to bed. In a short period of time, I started seeing my business bloom, creating more wealth for me and my family. It wasn't just my business that flourished, but also my health and happiness. Even my personal life took a wonderful turn that put my life on the path to abundance. I was wondering what was going on! Why was I seeing so much improvement in all aspects of life?

Meditation helps you connect with the higher power, and from that higher power, you can draw to you whatever you want. Everything exists within you. All the money, wealth, happiness and health that you're looking for is inside you. The simple practice of meditation made me realize this great truth of life. There's an inner world inside you. Whatever you feel inside is what you see in your outer world. Before all these exercises, I was trying to change my outside world to get more money and happiness, as well as good health and wealth. That's why I was always lacking in everything. Once meditation helped me discover my inner world, it helped me connect with the higher power. Then I got everything I was looking for in the outer world. That's the importance of making the connection with the beautiful world inside you. I get more and more aware every day, and the results I'm achieving due to this practice are phenomenal and mind-blowing. Most people are looking for wealth and money in the outside world, and that's why they're not finding it. They are unaware of their beautiful, marvelous inner world.

Once you realize that whatever you're feeling inside, you'll feel outside, it makes a huge difference. Whatever you want to achieve comes through changing your inner world. The results are automatic. Once you change your inner world and feel however you want, it will manifest in reality and in your physical world. Don't wait for the perfect moment; this moment is right in front of you. Realize the beautiful world inside you that's part of the universal mind. You won't lack anything when you do this. Your inside world, like nature, is abundant in everything. Look around at nature. Do you see any lack? No! Everything is abundant, the same way it is inside us. We just have to draw from this beautiful, bountiful and marvelous world. Get ready for your inner world to provide you with everything you want and desire! Just think about and imagine what you want. Life is a beautiful journey, so get on board! Don't waste this wonderful trip. Live fully, as you only have one life to live.

As I said, meditation helps to calm your mind and makes you more serene and peaceful. Start meditating today. Quiet your mind for three minutes. Then, a few days later, go to five minutes, and then seven minutes. I recommend meditating either first thing in the morning or before retiring for the day. It's made such a difference for me, and I'm sure it will create magic for you and help you achieve whatever you want in your life. It will make your dreams come true and help you see your dream life in reality sooner rather than later. Don't wait for the right time; the time is right when you take the first step. So, go for it! Manifest the life you're dreaming about and want to live. Life is waiting for you, so get started. In the meditative state, you'll be calm, serene, quiet, pure, and gracious. When we're meditating, we're not finding money – we're finding our "self." When you find yourself, you don't need anything else, because you are perfect, abundant, gracious, whole and complete the way God made you. God wants you to be successful, happy, healthy and abundant in all aspects of life. He wants you to enjoy all the luxuries of life. You are unique. Nobody is like you, so be yourself and discover your self, who is perfect, through this beautiful, loving, peaceful exercise of meditation.

Since I discovered myself, I am enjoying life to the fullest. I didn't do anything extraordinary. These simple rituals of self-discovery have made my life abundant, and they'll work for you, too. Be yourself. God made you perfect. You're his highest creation. You are brilliant, whole, and complete – but you have to see yourself from his perspective. From his creation, you have to discover yourself. These are the simple rituals I used that worked wonders for me and are still working for me. If these rituals can work for me, they'll work for anybody. By following these simple, easy-to-do rituals, I changed my life and went from lacking money to becoming a successful millionaire. You may think that money isn't everything, but it pervades most of your life. It's life's necessity; you can't live happily and enjoy life without money. Money buys the luxury life you're looking for, and it can let you be free in this life. God, who created us, wants us to be free and enjoy life to the fullest.

In life, we get stuck in our day-to-day activities and start running after things, and we forget to live this beautiful life. Every day, we are running after things we don't even need. We're running after things only to be competitive and feel better about ourselves in the eyes of somebody else. We have to be creative rather than competitive. When we're on a competitive frequency, we're thinking there's lack in the world. In reality, there is abundance everywhere. Wherever you look, you find abundance: in trees, the sea, the animals, and all monetary things. There's no scarcity in this world; it has everything you're looking for.

Your mind, which is the most powerful tool in this world, will help you achieve anything you choose. You just have to let the universe know what you really want. Most people don't know what they want. When they lack money and all the necessities and luxuries of life, they blame their circumstances and the people around them. They blame their country and the economy, but in reality, they don't even know what they're looking for. If you ask life for what you want, life will give you everything. On the other hand, if you don't know what you want from life, life has nothing to offer you. So, decide what you really want from this amazing life, and life will give you your dream life, your dream car, your dream partner, your dream house, or your dream business. You have to release it to the universe and let your higher power know your desires. You won't believe how easy it is to get everything you desire! People think it's complicated. They don't believe it can be as easy as following these simple rituals, which will bring health, happiness, abundance, wealth and prosperity into your life. They think it is too good to be true.

In my experience, at the top of my list is philosophy. If you change your philosophy, you can get everything in life. You have to start by working hard on yourself and becoming a better person. If you're working hard at your job and not doing anything to improve yourself, you're not going to get anywhere. You can live a good life that way, but you won't be able to live it to the fullest. As you work on yourself, don't think about what you're getting; think about what kind of person you're becoming. Success is not something you pursue; it's something you attract by becoming the person you want to be. For example, when I set a goal to earn a million dollars in a year, it wasn't the million dollars I earned by setting the goal that mattered. During the process of achieving that goal, the person I became is priceless. You can always lose a million dollars, but by becoming the type of person who can attract it, you can always achieve it again. I feel so blessed to know about this philosophy of life by following so many great teachers like Jim Rohn, Bob Proctor, Jack Canfield, Tony Robbins and Earl Nightingale. I am indebted to these great teachers.

In my opinion, life is beautiful. You have to figure out why you're here by yourself. You're mainly here to enjoy every bit of it. God (or the higher power/infinite power which is within you), wants you to enjoy every aspect of life to the fullest. He wants you to be happy, healthy and wealthy. He supplied you with all the faculties to achieve success, happiness, abundance, and prosperity. You have to use these faculties to achieve what your heart desires and what you want to be in this life. The sky's the limit for man, the highest creation of God. We have a wonderful and most amazing power that no other living species has: that of creative imagination. With creative imagination, you can do anything by seeing the images in your mind.

I'd like to tell you from the depth of my heart that these little rituals which I've done every day for the last two and a half years have really helped me achieve success, abundance and happiness in my life. About two and a half years ago, I was trying to figure out how to make more money and have more time for my family and to travel. I thought I could only make money by working hard and working more hours. There are only 24 hours in a day. What can you do in that time? When I found the secret, it became much easier to make money and do the things I'd always wanted to do, and I went on vacation more often. During the first six months of my results, I wondered why, all of a sudden, I was making more money, having more time off and traveling more. Then I attended the "Paradigm Shift Seminar" in Los Angeles given by Bob Proctor and Sandy Gallagher. All the puzzle pieces fell into place. I understood why I was becoming that which I am today. I was looking for all the same things you are. That's why you're reading this book. As I explained, during this time of my self-discovery, I listened to self-help tapes every day. I was reading every day for at least thirty minutes and watching positive self-help videos on YouTube. All those things changed my self-image, which resulted in freedom. I am so grateful for all the abundance I'm receiving by doing these simple day-to-day rituals. If you're looking to turn your life around, these simple rituals are the way to do it.

Here's a reminder of the most important steps to take:

- Find out what you really want in your life

- Write your goals down on a piece of paper, and say them aloud every day

- Don't think about how you're going to achieve them. Leave that job to the higher power.

- The higher power will guide you if you believe.

- The higher power will show you the path to freedom, abundance and happiness

- The higher power will bring all the right people and circumstances into your life to take you toward your goals and your dream life

Your part is to decide what you want and believe that it's possible to start living the life you want to live.

The sky is the limit. Go for your dreams, and I'm sure they'll come true!

Good luck!

I've never met you, but I feel like I already know you and will see you fulfilling your dreams and living the life you always imagined. You just didn't know the secret, but now you do – so what are you waiting for?

Your dream life is waiting for you…

Think…Imagine…Feel…Live.

Life is the art of discovering new ways to live fully to your potential, which is unlimited.

Let other people lead small and limited lives, but not you. You were born to succeed. Your bright future is in your hands. Don't leave it in someone else's hands.

Some people have learned to earn large amounts, but they've never learned the art of living. Find a way to earn well and live well. Balance and harmony is what everybody needs in life.

Life cannot be measured. It is living purposefully with ambition in mind. It will take you where you imagine in your mind. It's a game you should practice well and know the rules to play. Once you know the rules, it will become a dream ride.

Start acting and living your dream life today, at this moment. It will unfold beyond your imagination.

Thank you very much for reading this book. Good luck on your journey to abundance, health, wealth, joy, happiness and prosperity.

Thank you so much.

With great gratitude,
Dr. Varinder Mann

ABOUT THE AUTHOR

Dr. Varinder Mann is a veterinarian running a successful veterinary hospital in California, where he lives with his wife and beautiful daughters, Avi and Mannat. He has a passion for animals and helps relieve the pain of beloved pets daily. Mann is a student of personal development, and has attended motivational seminars and worked with Jack Canfield, Bob Proctor and Tony Robbins. He's also a success coach and certified consultant in Jack Canfield's "Train the Trainer" Program. In his spare time, he likes to read, write and travel. He has two dogs named Oscar and Fliur, and one cat named Una.

For more information on Dr. Varinder Mann
please contact
manndvm37@gmail.com

With every donation, a voice will be given to the creativity that lies within the hearts of our children living with diverse challenges.

By making this difference, children that may not have been given the opportunity to have their Heart Heard will have the freedom to create beautiful works of art and musical creations.

Donate by visiting

HeartstobeHeard.com

We thank you.